START

Thinking

Bugs and Slugs

Terry Jennings

QEB Publishing, Inc.

Copyright © QEB Publishing, Inc. 2005

Published in the United States by
QEB Publishing, Inc.
23062 La Cadena Drive
Laguna Hills, CA 92653
www.qeb-publishing.com

Library of Congress Control Number: 2005921163

ISBN 1-59566-069-0

Written by Terry Jennings
Designed by Caroline Grimshaw
Editor Hannah Ray
Picture Researcher Nic Dean

Series Consultant Anne Faundez
Publisher Steve Evans
Creative Director Louise Morley
Editorial Manager Jean Coppendale

Printed and bound in China

Picture credits

Key: t = top, b = bottom, m = middle, l = left, r = right

ardea.com/Steve Hopkin 14, 20r; **Butterfly Conservation Picture Library** 7, 8, 9, 19r, 22tr, 22tl;
Corbis/George McCarthy 5b, /Wolfgang Kaehier 6, /Ken Wilson; Papillo 10, /Darrell Gulin 11, 19l,
/Robert Pickett 12, 20l, /Ralph A. Clevenger 18l; **Ecoscene**/Robin Williams 13, /Robert Pickett 17, 21r, 22b;
Getty Images/ Greg Johnston/Lonely Planet Images 4, /Derek P. Redfearn/The Image Bank 16, 21l, 22bl;
photolibrary.com/Kathie Atkinson/Oxford Scientific 15; **Still Pictures**/Hans Pfletschinger 5t, 18r, 22m.

With thanks to Butterfly Conservation

Contents

Small animals are everywhere

Grasshopper

Bee

Snail

There are many different kinds of small animals. You can see them everywhere—in your backyard, in a park or garden, or in your school playground.

How many small animals can you find?

You may have to look hard to see them!

Insects

Bees, wasps, flies, moths, ants, and beetles are all types of **insect**.

There are thousands of kinds of insect in the world.

Rhinoceros beetle

Butterfly

All insects have six legs, and many have wings. Wasps and moths have four wings, but flies only have two wings. Even some ants have wings.

Butterflies are also insects. They lay their eggs on plants.

A caterpillar **hatches** from each egg and starts to eat the leaves of the plant.

When the caterpillar has eaten enough, it turns into a **chrysalis**.

The chrysalis does not move or eat, but amazing changes happen inside it.

Inside the chrysalis, the caterpillar turns into a butterfly.

Spiders

Spiders have eight legs, which means they are not insects. They live among plants and in buildings.

Most spiders make a sticky web.
When an insect flies into the web,
it becomes trapped. The spider
rushes out. It wraps up the insect
in sticky thread, ready to eat later.

Woodlice

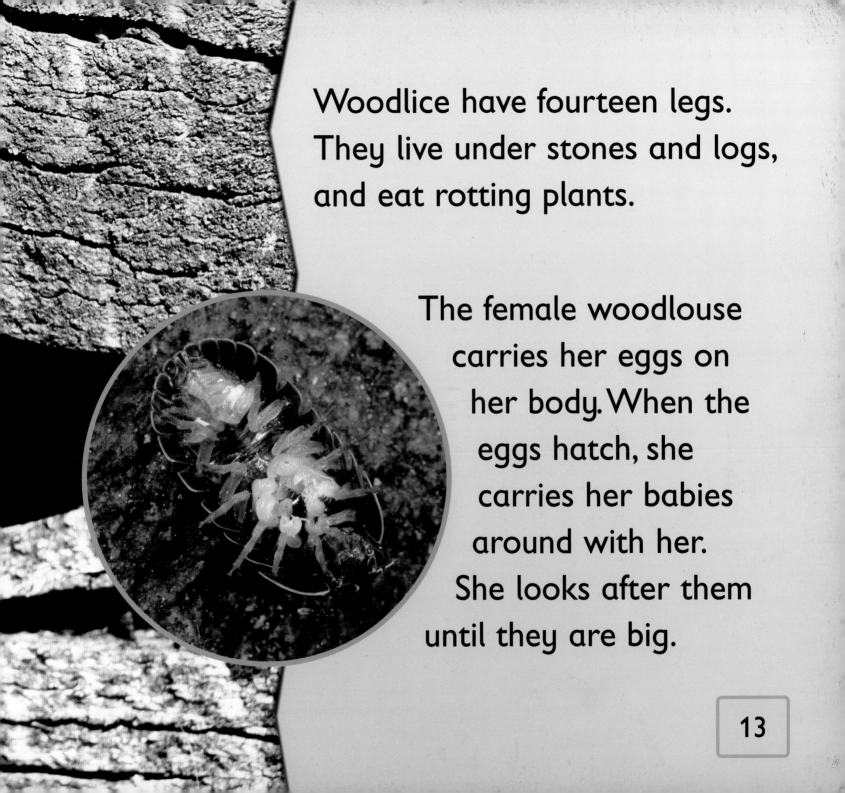

Woodlice have fourteen legs. They live under stones and logs, and eat rotting plants.

The female woodlouse carries her eggs on her body. When the eggs hatch, she carries her babies around with her. She looks after them until they are big.

Earthworms

An earthworm's body is made up of rings, called segments.

14

Each segment
has tiny bristles
on it which help
the worm to
move along.

Earthworms
live in the
soil and eat
rotting leaves.

Earthworms
lay eggs, which
hatch into
tiny worms.

15

Snails and slugs

A snail has a **shell** on its back. When the weather is cold or dry, the snail stays in its shell.

16

Slugs are like snails, but they do not have a shell. Both slugs and snails make **slimy** trails as they move. This helps them slide along smoothly.

Both snails and slugs eat plants and rotting leaves.

How can you tell if an animal is an insect?

Can you name three different types of insect?

18

What does a
caterpillar turn into?

What is a spider's
web used for?

How can you tell
that a woodlouse
is not an insect?

What helps an earthworm
move along?

What is the difference between a slug and a snail?

When does a snail go into its shell?

Glossary

Chrysalis—the stage between being a caterpillar and a butterfly or moth.

Hatch—to break out of an egg.

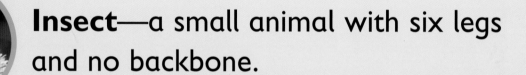

Insect—a small animal with six legs and no backbone.

Shell—the thin, hard part around an egg, a nut, or some kinds of animals, such as snails.

Slime—a wet, slippery substance.

22

Index

23

Parents' and teachers' notes

- Look at the front cover of the book together. Read the title and look at the picture. Can your child guess what the book is going to be about?
- Look through the book. How many of the animals in the photographs can your child recognize? Can your child think of any more small creatures?
- Read through the book together. Tell your child that the words in **bold** are explained in the glossary on page 22. Look up each word in bold as you encounter it.
- Using the glossary definition of the word "insect," and the information within the book itself, make sets of those animals which are insects and those which are not.
- Look for small animals by carefully turning over logs and stones. Be sure to replace the logs or stones exactly as they were. Discuss why small animals like to hide in these places.
- Let your child practice using a magnifying glass to examine small animals.

- Make a wallchart of pictures of insects and other types of minibeasts, to show the great variety of form, structure, and color.
- On a hot day, sit quietly by a flowerbed with your child. Watch to see which kinds of insects visit the flowers. Which color flowers does each insect go to? (Do not go too close to bees or try to touch them.)
- Make up a story about "the ladybug who was different" (some are yellow with black spots, while others are black with red spots).
- Visit a zoo, wildlife park, or butterfly house and look at exotic invertebrates, including tropical spiders.
- Choose another minibeast (for example, a stick insect, ladybug, or ant). Discuss what you already know about this creature. Together, research your chosen animal and write a factsheet on it. Encourage your child to draw some pictures to accompany the text.
- Does your child have a favorite minibeast? Why is this creature his or her favorite?

24